with Warm
Heart and
Receptive
Mind

with Warm Heart and Receptive Mind

A Compendium of 101 Sayings and Quotations on the Themes of Compassion and Education

Collected and Edited by Bill Gent

In collaboration with

BEACON BOOKS

THE COED FOUNDATION

First published in the UK by Beacon Books and Media Ltd
Innospace, Chester Street, Manchester M1 5GD, UK.

First paperback edition published 2018
Printed in the UK
www.beaconbooks.net

Cataloging-in-Publication record for this book is available from the
British Library

ISBN 978-1-912356-13-3

Cover design by Bipin Mistry
Front cover photo by Aaron Burden on Unsplash

Publishing credits
Every effort has been made by the editor and publisher to trace copyright
holders and to obtain their permission for the use of copyright material. The
publisher apologizes for any errors or omissions in the following list and would
be grateful if notified of any corrections that should be incorporated in future
reprints or editions of this book. The following people, publishers and bodies are
thanked for agreeing to grant such permission: Independent Thinking Press (3);
Janet Scott (8); I B Taurus Publishers (13); Egmont (16); Values Based Education
(17); W W Norton(22); Edinburgh University Press (29); Jessica Kingsley publishers (31); Britain Yearly Meeting of the Religious Society of Friends (Quakers)
in Britain (30); Jubilee Centre for Character and Virtues (49); SPCK (22, 35);
Bloomsbury Publishing Plc (34, 38, 67, 82); McGraw Hill Education (79, 88);
The Random House Group Limited (11, 53, 78); Routledge (93).

Contents

Acknowledgements

Most of the sayings reproduced in this book are taken from my own collection of sayings and proverbs which I have been gathering, on and off, for the last 40 years or so. Others were sent to me by colleagues and friends once they heard that this new collection was underway. As such, my thanks go to: Mel Woodcock (36), Andrew Peterson (18, 22), Mary Myatt (60), David Woods (33, 81, 50), Alan Brine (4), Peter McCarthy (38), Steve Green (6), Ruth Finnegan (95, 46, 31) Maurice Irfan Coles (24, 58, 64, 101), Jenny Berglund (56), Eve Collis (7, 32, 100). My thanks also go to those who so willingly chased up the sources of particular quotations and sayings for me, particularly Richard Pring (26).

I am also very grateful to fellow trustees and advisers of the charity 'The Compassion in Education Foundation' for helping me to make a selection from the several draft collections which I asked them to look through and to indicate which sayings in particular 'spoke' to them.

Ultimately, of course, the decision to include a specific saying rested with me as editor and, as such, if they either 'turn you on' or 'turn you off', the responsibility for inclusion rests solely with me.

Bill Gent
Editor

Foreword

Like so many people who have spent their lives in and around schools I have never been able to resist quotations. Bill Gent has assembled here a treasure chest, discarding countless others which might be in your choice of 101. But you will find a fair few here which will make you think again.

Good schools use quotations as ingredients in creating an environment fit for learning, whether through 'Quote for the Week' which, displayed in the hall, becomes the theme for an assembly or through the Plasma rolling screen of school images in reception. Perhaps my favourite is a south London comprehensive school. Consider:

A visit to the school revealed the familiar flat roofs, rotting wood and disintegrating window frames of a school, system-built in a hurry in the 1960s. My visit was before the announcement of Building Schools for the Future. (It's easy to forget how we were depressingly resigned to teaching in schools like this year after year with no sign of the cavalry on the horizon. And, as we now sadly realise, the cavalry has gone again, so this story may have a resonance for some schools abandoned by the cancellation of BSF or indeed any school determined to attend to the possibilities of enhancing the educational impact of their environment.) Anyway, on entry, one was struck by the extraordinary way in which the school was a visually stimulating delight, despite its building. This was partly because there seemed to be hundreds of thought-provoking, uplifting and beautifully framed quotations scattered around the walls of dining hall and corridors. Quotations such as this:

> 'History says don't hope on this side of the grave.
> Then once in a lifetime
> The longed-for tidal wave of justice can rise up
> When Hope and History rhyme.' (*Seamus Heaney*)
> Presented by Jade Smith, Year 9

When asked, the Head explained in an off-hand way "Oh it's 'quid for a quote'" before elaborating how he and his deputies went to each of the Year assemblies in September and with the Head of Year spoke, vividly no doubt, about quotations they personally liked. The tutors did the same and had framed and displayed their own favourites in the class base. The first homework of the year was to discuss with the family and come back with five well-liked quotations. ("We asked for five because we thought at least one would be ok. And we promised that if one were thought worthy of framing and hanging, we would send"—and he said this with a wink—"£1 home to give to their favourite charity".) And so, with a little bit of help from Design and Technology, 1,300 framed quotations were duly hung around the school. It cost £3,000 in total and the environment was transformed.

So, here's a special collection reminding you that Coleridge was right when he called language,

> 'the armoury of the human mind where it stores the
> trophies of its past and the weapons of its future conquests.'

Sir Tim Brighouse
Former Schools Commissioner for London

Introduction

Living in today's economically developed societies, it is easy to forget just how word-filled and text-filled our everyday worlds are. Indeed, it is easy to forget just what a historic and significant invention writing (and later, printing) was. For, as the American scholar of literacy, Walter Ong has said, 'More than any other single invention, writing has transformed human consciousness'.[1] Even in societies where literacy was traditionally the gift of the few, the image of writing and the book seeped into people's minds. Take, for instance, the profound African proverb, 'When an old person dies, a library burns'.

And here I go ... I am trying to introduce a book of sayings and statements and, in the very process of doing so, am resorting to quoting the words and sayings of others!

The truth is that, over the centuries, people have frequently used the words of others to pepper and improve their own verbal or written outpourings. Just take, for example, the case of that universal category of saying, the 'proverb'. The proverb, once defined as 'The wit of one and the wisdom of many'[2] (there I go again!), is a phenomenon that is found across all cultures and historical eras. Indeed, proverbs have been the focus of a vast academic literature, the study of proverbs being known as 'paremiology'.

And, to bring these thoughts back to the everyday, I defy you to walk down any town or city street and not come across a myriad of ways in which the consumer society has sought to utilise sayings and statements in order to attract interest and, in the process, to boost sales. And, to jog your memory and concentrate your attention, consider the following five examples: on mugs (I have one that has Oscar Wilde's dictum 'I have nothing to declare but my genius' running around its rim); on plaques to hang inside or outside the home (contemporary garden centres are a treasure trove of these); bumper stickers on cars (including the well-known, 'If you can read this, thank a teacher'); on t-shirts (just last week, I walked behind a man who had printed on the back of his t-shirt, the opening words of the Jewish and Christian Bible, 'In the beginning, God created the heavens and the earth...'); and, finally, on shopping bags (particularly those provided by booksellers).

And this is only on the street! Move inside buildings into offices and places where people work and gather and you will begin to see—once you have trained your eyes to identify this phenomenon—sayings and statements, varying in quality and appropriateness, displayed in all kinds of locations: on notice boards, on the edge of computer screens, on walls and windows, and on the front of diaries. Visiting a school bursar some time ago, for example, I was amused by the following statement pinned to her notice board: 'Some days the best thing about my job is that the chair swivels'. Waiting in a dentist's queue, on the other hand, I was fascinated by a wall poster that consisted of a beautiful seascape upon which had been superimposed, 'The larger the island of knowledge, the longer the shoreline of wonder'.[3] And, on a visit to a local museum, I looked at the mock-up of a Victorian schoolroom which had, written in copperplate writing on the blackboard, the well-known proverb (ready for the students to copy, we surmise), 'Too many cooks spoil the broth'.

But, more than this, I once had a colleague whose wallet was full of little bits of paper on to which he had written sayings and statements that had attracted him for some reason. Over a coffee break, he was sometimes wont to share his latest acquisitions with others. Some people, as I do, have been collecting sayings and statements for decades,[4] first written into notebooks and now stored digitally. Indeed, some collectors have had extracts from their collections published.[5] Historically, this penchant for collecting all sorts of 'telling' sayings and statements—including poems, proverbs, quotations from writings, personal thoughts and reflections—has led many people to compile what are known as 'commonplace books'. Annie, the eldest daughter of Charles Darwin, for example, maintained a number of still extant commonplace books into one of which she recorded the following charming little poem: 'It cometh forth in April showers, lies snug when storms prevail; it feeds on fruits; it sleeps on flowers; I would I were a snail!'[6]

All of this, of course, gives rise to the underlying question: what is it about sayings and statements (in their multiple forms such as quotations, aphorisms, proverbs, adages, epigrams, inscriptions and epigraphs) that make them so memorable, attractive and collectible? Bearing in mind the old adage that 'To every complex question there is a simple answer—that is wrong!', this question can give rise to long and discursive answers.[7] Suffice it here to say that suggestions might include: their attractiveness so that they play on our mind; their memorability; their elegance and/or economy of wording; the authority which they extend to the words of others; their capacity to put into words what we have often been striving to express ourselves; and—often at their very heart—their wit and wisdom.

What follows in this book is a collection of sayings and statements—ranging from pithy one-liners to solid quotations—that have a bearing on the themes of compassion and education. They emerge from the work of a group of trustees and advisers associated with the charity 'The CoED Foundation'—a leading voice for compassion in education—which was founded by Maurice Irfan Coles in 2012. The group is varied in both background and experience but all are committed to ensuring that—under a deluge of educational 'reform' over recent decades and an increasing demand to define educational success almost exclusively in terms of measurable and statistical outcomes—sight is not lost of the intensely personal and humanitarian nature of schooling and education. Indeed, so profoundly and intensely do so many people feel this that it is often only in a profound, erudite or ironic statement that these beliefs are captured. It was in the Foundation's idea of gathering together such a collection of statements and sayings that the origins of this book lay.

We hope that readers will find the collection at least interesting and perhaps even stirring. And those of you who are currently involved in educational activity might just find even more practical uses for particular statements or sayings: as a focus of a school assembly; as a space-filler on a notice board; as a school 'thought for the week'; as a part of a 'wall of wisdom'[8] in a classroom; as a personal reminder to tuck into your purse or wallet. Or you might even choose to follow in the footsteps of the great French essay-writer, Montaigne (1533-1592),[9] who reputedly tracked down sayings and aphorisms and inscribed them on the ceiling of his study.

Bill Gent
Frinton-on-Sea, Essex
1.1.2018

References

[1] Ong, W J (1982), *Orality and Literacy: The Technologizing of the Word* (London: Methuen) 78.

[2] This was the definition supplied by Lord John Russell in the mid-nineteenth century. Cited in: Mieder, W (1999) 'Popular Views of the Proverb' in *De Proverbio* 5:2.

[3] Attributed to Ralph W Sockman, US pastor (1889-1970).

[4] In his autobiography, the British philosopher of religion and theologian, John Hick, recorded that at the age of 18 he kept 'a notebook of philosophical reflections, aphorisms, a literary form learned from Nietzsche': Hick, J (2002) *John Hick: an autobiography* (Oxford: Oneworld), 32.

[5] See, for example: Magnus Magnusson's *Keeping My Words: an anthology from cradle to grave* (London: Hodder & Stoughton, 2004) and John G Murray's *A Gentleman Publisher's Commonplace Book* (London: John Murray, 1996).

[6] Keynes, R (2002) *Darwin, His Daughter & Human Evolution* (New York: Riverhead), 109.

[7] See, for example: Finnegan, R (2011) *Why Do We Quote? The Culture and History of Quotations* (Cambridge: Open Book Publishers).

[8] A board on which fascinating or challenging sayings and questions—including those that come from the mouths of students during lessons—are displayed for the interest and rumination of others. The phrase 'wall of wisdom' was coined by Anne Krisman.

[9] Higgins, G (2000) *Porcupines: A Philosophical Anthology* (London: Penguin) xvii.

.

— 1 —

Dear brothers and sisters, we must not forget that millions of people are suffering from poverty and injustice and ignorance. We must not forget that millions of children are out of their schools. We must not forget that our sisters and brothers are waiting for a bright, peaceful future. So let us wage a glorious struggle against illiteracy, poverty and terrorism, let us pick up our books and our pens, they are the most powerful weapons. One child, one teacher, one book and one pen can change the world. Education is the only solution. Education first.

16 year-old Malala Yousafzai,
speaking at the UN, New York, July 2013

This speech, at the first ever Youth Takeover of the United Nations, was widely reported throughout the world. Both text and film record are available on the Internet. In October 2014, Malala Yousafzai, together with Kailash Satyarthi, was awarded the Nobel Peace prize.

2

School should be, for the less fortunate,
what home is for the more fortunate.
A place where there is work but also laughter,
a place where there is law but also grace,
a place where there is justice but
where there is also love.

Sir Alec Clegg (1909-1984)

Sir Alec Clegg, Chief Education Officer of the West Riding of Yorkshire (1945-1974), was a powerful advocate of comprehensive education in his day. This quotation, dated 1974 but with no source given, can be found at the head of the 'discipline and behaviour policy' of Market Field School in Essex (www.marketfieldschool. co.uk/policies, accessed 6.1.17)

3

Schools are fascinating and busy places and there is much that happens in them that is very funny and sometimes absurd. One of the sadder aspects of recent years is that teachers and others who work in schools seem to have less time to laugh with the children and each other at some of the amusing things that happen. Childhood should be joyous and schools should feel part of that happy outlook.

Mick Waters, British educationalist

Waters, M (2013) *Thinking Allowed on Schooling* (Carmarthen: Independent Thinking Press), p3. Professor Mick Waters, a trustee of the CoED Foundation, was Director of Curriculum at the (British) Qualifications and Curriculum Authority (QCA), 2005-2009.

~❧ 4 ❧~

*Your children are not your children. They are the
sons and daughters of Life's longing for itself.
They come through you but not from you,
And though they are with you yet
they belong not to you.*

Kahlil Gibran, *The Prophet*

Gibran, Kahlil, *The Prophet* (London: William Heinemann), p20.
This short book, written by the Lebanese-American poet and artist
Kahlil Gibran and first published in 1923, has influenced many who
believe that its poetic words present images and intuitions of great
profundity.

5

Children are not the people of tomorrow, but are people of today. They have a right to be taken seriously, and to be treated with tenderness and respect. They should be allowed to grow into whoever they were meant to be – the unknown person inside each of them is our hope for the future.

Janusz Korczak, Polish educator,
author, paediatrician (1872-1942)

It is the final act of Janusz Korczak (pronounced Kor-chok) that is often know best to others – his death with 200 children from the Warsaw orphanage where he worked at Treblinka extermination camp in 1942. This statement is cited in: Joseph, S (Ed) *Loving Every Child: Wisdom for Parents: The Words of Janusz Korczak.*

6

You are the women who will build the world as it should be. You're going to write the next chapter in history. Not just for yourselves, but for your generation and generations to come. And that's why getting a good education is so important. That's why all of this that you're going through – the ups and the downs, the teachers that you love and the teachers that you don't – why it's so important.

Michelle Obama speaking to an audience of girls at a London secondary school, April 2009

Michelle Obama, First Lady of the United States, gave the talk from which this extract is taken at Elizabeth Garrett Anderson School, a girls' comprehensive school in Islington, London, in April 2009. The school displays the opening sentence on its website. See www.ted.com/talks/michelle_obama (accessed 25.12.16).

7

If you want to build a ship, don't drum up people together to collect wood and don't assign them tasks and work, but rather teach them to long for the sea.

Antoine de Saint-Exupéry (1900-1944),
French author and aviator

Investigation has shown that it is impossible to attribute this quotation in this form to any of the works of Saint-Exupéry. It is probably based on an English paraphrase of a statement in French in one of the author's works.

8

A teacher has to combine the love of the subject with the love of the pupil and have the humility that puts the flourishing of both before their own ego. Above all, teachers are examples of what they want their pupils to be. They teach through who they are and through what they do.

Janet Scott, British Quaker and educationalist

From Cambridge University sermon preached by Janet Scott, 1.2.2015; private copy supplied by Janet Scott, June 2015.

9

Teachers open our eyes to the world. They give us curiosity and confidence. They teach us to ask questions. They connect us to our past and future. They are the guardians of our social heritage... Life without a teacher is simply not a life.

Rabbi Jonathan Sacks, British Jewish author

Sacks, J (2000) *The Politics of Hope* (London: Vintage), p71. Jonathan Sacks, a most gifted writer and commentator, was Chief Rabbi of the Hebrew Congregations of the Commonwealth, 1991-2013.

10

No man is an island entire of itself;
every man is a piece of the continent, a part of the
main; if a clod be washed away by the sea, Europe
is the less, as well as if a promontory were, as well
as any manner of thy friends or of thine own
were; any man's death diminishes me, because I am
involved in mankind. And therefore never send to
know for whom the bell tolls;
it tolls for thee.

John Donne, English metaphysical poet (1572-1631)

Meditation 17 of his prose work, *Devotions Upon Emergent Questions* (1624).

—⨎ 11 ⨏—

Our humanity is caught up in that of all others.
We are human because we belong. We are made
for community, for togetherness, for family, to
exist in a delicate network of interdependence.

Desmond Tutu, South African Christian leader

Tutu, D (1999), *No Future Without Forgiveness*, (London: Rider), p154. See notes on p77 for comment on the African concept of Ubuntu.

⟋⟋ 12 ⟋⟋

There are people whose presence is encouraging.
One of the most beautiful gifts in the world is the
gift of encouragement. When someone encourages
you, they help you cross a threshold you might
otherwise never have crossed on your own.

John O'Donohue, Irish poet and author (1956-2008)

O'Donohue, John (2000), *Eternal Echoes: Exploring Our Hunger to Belong* (London: Bantam Books), pp88-89.

13

I strongly believe that the purpose of all learning should be about changing oneself and thereby the world in some small way.

Mona Siddiqui, British Muslim academic

Siddiqui, Mona (2015) *My Way: A Muslim Woman's Journey* (London: I B Taurus), p111. Many radio listeners first came across the name of Mona Siddiqui through her regular contribution to BBC Radio 4 Today Programme's 'Thought for the Day'.

— 14 —

Learning is the best type of wealth.
It is easy to carry with you.
Thieves can't steal it.
Bullies can't take it from you.
Water and fire can't destroy it.
When you share your learning
It grows instead of getting less.

5th century Tamil poem

For well over ten years, I was privileged to have a 'Thought for the Week' slot in the weekly education newsletter that was sent out in the outer London borough in which I worked. This was one of my offerings but, sadly, I can no longer trace its source.

15

Soap and education are not as sudden as a massacre,
but they are more deadly in the long run.

Mark Twain, US author (1835-1910)

Collections of memorable quotations usually include a fair number from the mind and pen of Mark Twain. This statement comes from an ironic and amusing essay, written under the guise of 'clerk to of the Senate Committee on Conchology', that he wrote in 1867: *The Facts Concerning The Present Resignation.*

16

Those who have no compassion have no wisdom.
Knowledge, yes; cleverness, maybe; wisdom, no.
A clever mind is not a heart.
Knowledge doesn't really care.
Wisdom does.

Benjamin Hoff, US author

Benjamin Hoff (2015), *The Tao of Pooh and the Te of Piglet* (London: Egmont), p14.

Compassion is the understanding that we are not perfect and we all make mistakes. We all struggle at times to be the best that we can be. We all fail at times to act as we would like. Compassion is accepting this in ourselves and in people with whom we are in relationship. Compassion is the gift of care to others and to ourselves.

From The Relationship Quotient: Creating Successful Relationships

Hendry J, Hawkes N, Fuller A, (2016) 'The Relationship Quotient', www.generationnext.com.au / www.valuesbasededucation.com

— ⟋ *18* ⟍ —

*It is the supreme art of the teacher to awaken
joy in creative expression and knowledge.*

Albert Einstein, physicist, philosopher, Nobel Prize winner
(1879-1955)

The translation of the German words placed on a plaque when
Einstein dedicated the astronomy building at Pasadena City College
in 1931. It is not certain, though probable, that the words were
coined by Einstein himself.

—⟐ 19 ⟐—

Creativity relies on the flow of ideas. This happens best in an atmosphere where risk is encouraged, playfulness with ideas is accepted and where failure is not punished but seen as part of the process of success.

Ken Robinson, British educationalist

Robinson, K (2001), *Out of Our Minds: Learning to Be Creative*, (London: Capstone), pp189-190. Ken Robinson, Professor Emeritus of the University of Warwick, now lives in the US. He is a renowned and entertaining speaker, his TED talk on 'Do schools kill creativity?' (2006) being viewed over 13 million times. www.ted.com/talks/ken_robinson_says_schools_kill_creativity

20

I can imagine no greater satisfaction for a person,
in looking back on his life and work, than to have
been able to give some people, however few, a feeling
of genuine pride in belonging to the human species
and, beyond that, a zestful yen to justify that pride.

Norman Cousins, US political journalist (1915–1990)

Cousins, Norman (1980) *Human Options: An Autobiographical Notebook.*

21

The nature of relationships among the adults within a school has a greater influence on the character and quality of that school and on student accomplishment than anything else.

Roland S Barth, US educator

Barth, Roland S (2006) *'Improving Relationships Within the Schoolhouse'* in *Educational Leadership*, 63:6, 8-13. Roland Barth is well-known for his espousal of collegiality and the need to share 'craft knowledge'.

22

*Mark would come into the room and, without
any fuss, would start talking about whatever
what was to be talked about. Most of the time he
asked questions. His questions were very good,
and if you tried to answer them intelligently, you
found yourself saying excellent things that you
did not know you knew, and that you had not,
in fact, known before. ... His classes were literally
'education' —they brought things out of you, they
made your mind produce its own explicit ideas.*

Thomas Merton (1915-1968) on one of his own teachers

Merton, Thomas (1975), *The Seven Storey Mountain* (London: Sheldon Press) p139. The 'Mark' that Thomas Merton was referring to was Mark Van Doren, a teacher at Columbia University, New York, who taught Merton in the mid-1930s.

23

I like a teacher who gives you something to take home to think about besides homework.

Lily Tomlin ('Edith Ann'), US comic actress

Cited in: Magnusson, Magnus (2004) *Keeping My Words: An Anthology from Cradle to Grave* (London: Hodder & Stoughton), p73.

— 24 —

*If we want to grow as teachers—we must do
something alien to academic culture: we must talk
to each other about our inner lives—risky stuff
in a profession that fears the personal and seeks
safety in the technical, the distant, the abstract.*

Parker J Palmer, US educator

Palmer, Parker J (1998) *The Courage to Teach: Exploring the Inner Landscape of a Teacher's Life*, (San Francisco: Jossey Boss Publishers), p12. Parker J Palmer is a founder and senior partner of the Centre for Courage and Renewal in Seattle, Washington, USA.

~~ 25 ~~

Children in our culture need to be taught how to be aware of their own inner experience and their potential to be aware. It is only when we discover that we have such a thing as inner experience that we are able to respect it in other people.

David Hay, British researcher and author

David Hay (d.2014) was a pioneering British researcher into the study of contemporary reports of religious experience and the link between spirituality and well-being. Hay, D (1990) *Religious Experience Today: Studying the Facts* (London: Mowbray), pp106-7.

26

Dear Teacher
I am a survivor of a concentration camp.
My eyes saw what no man should witness:
Gas chambers built by learned engineers;
Children poisoned by educated physicians;
Infants killed by trained nurses;
Women and babies shot and burned by
high school and college graduates.
So, I am suspicious of education.
My request is:
Help your students become human.
Your efforts must never produce learned monsters,
skilled psychopaths, educated Eichmans.
Reading, writing, arithmetic are important only if
they serve to make our children more human.

The letter of a New York high school principal that she writes to
all new teachers, setting out the agenda for the school

Quoted in: Strom, M S (1981) *Facing History and Ourselves: Holocaust and Human Behaviour* (Waterdown, Mass: Intentional Education, p4.) I first came across this moving statement in the text of Richard Pring's Oxford University Sermon delivered in February 1993. I am grateful to Professor Pring, who told me that he met the Principal in person during a visit to New York, for tracing the publication source for me.

Dear Parents

The exams of your children are to start soon. I know you are all really anxious for your child to do well. But please do remember, amongst the students who will take the exams is an artist who doesn't need to understand Maths. There's an entrepreneur who doesn't care about History or English Literature. There's a musician whose Chemistry marks won't matter. There's a sportsperson whose physical fitness is more important than Physics.

If your child does get top marks, then great. But, if he or she doesn't, then don't take away their self-confidence from them. Tell them it's OK, it's just an exam. They are cut out for much bigger things in life. Tell them, no matter what they score, you love them and will not judge them.

Please do this and, if you do, watch your children conquer the world. One exam or a 90 per cent won't take away their dreams and talent.

A letter sent home to parents by a school in India

Like many much-copied sayings and quotations, a look on the internet will show that there are variant readings and a number of ascribed sources, including 'A principal in Singapore' and 'the Heritage School, Kolkata'.

28

To me it seems clear that a good school is one that is constantly engaged in self-examination, in improving itself, in becoming wiser in its ability to teach and inspire. It's a school that is intent on turning out good people who will make a better world. It's a school where ideas and ideals are in everyday circulation, the coinage of ordinary transactions.

Robert Lawrence Smith, US headteacher

Smith, Robert Lawrence (1998) *A Quaker Book of Wisdom: Life Lessons in Simplicity, Service and Common Sense* (London: Victor Gollancz), pp124-125.

—⟋ 29 ⟍—

The biggest challenge to information users in the cyber age is to find the right filters to separate the gems of knowledge from the piles of useless information.

Ebrahim Moosa, US academic

Moosa, Ebrahim (2015) *What Is a Madrasa?* (Edinburgh: Edinburgh University Press), p129.

─❦ *30* ❦─

*To "know oneself" as a teacher implies
acknowledging one's weaknesses, source of
prejudices and tendencies to stereotype. It involves
accepting one's effect on pupils and their parents.
Diagnosing a child's learning needs involves risking
being wrong. We can only see clearly and risk being
wrong when we have a high level of self-esteem
and when we love ourselves enough to be open.*

Sarah Worster (1988)

Britain Yearly Meeting. Quaker faith & practice. Fifth edition. London: The Yearly Meeting of the Religious Society of Friends (Quakers) in Britain, 2013. 23.77. © 2013

～✑ 31 ✑～

The question, 'Who am I?'
is often misinterpreted as,
'What do I do?'
We have become human doings
rather than human beings.

Adams K, Hyde B, Woolley R (2008), *The Spiritual Dimension*
of Childhood

Adams K, Hyde B, Woolley R (2008), *The Spiritual Dimension of Childhood* (London: Jessica Kingsley), p48.

I offer you my four Hs of leadership:

Humility: there are 7 billion people in the world as important as you are;
Humanity: every child really does matter and needs to be cared for;
Hope: every leader needs to be an optimist and believe that all children can succeed;
Humour: humour is the sine qua non of school leadership.

John Dunford, English headteacher and educationalist

Dunford, John (2012) *Senior Leadership: what does success look like?* (Nottingham: National College for School Leadership), p3. Sir John Dunford is currently the chair of the Whole Education organisation.

33

What are the broadest purposes of education—
to create a deeper sense of what is worth
in the 21st century, a deeper humanity?
In pursuing this endeavour you need
soul, suffering and above all, hope.

Professor Jonathan Jansen, South African educationalist

Though this saying was passed onto me and attributed to Professor Jonathan Jansen's *Leading Against the Grain*, I have been unable to trace its exact source. Jonathan Jansen is Vice-Chancellor and Rector at the University of the Free State and President of the South African Institute of Race Relations.

~ 34 ~

In order to compete with the world's best our young people will need to be adaptable and independent-minded, based on the secure foundation of well-established skills and knowledge; but they will also need to be creative thinkers and doers; and, for all our sakes, we need them to be socially aware, compassionate, community-builders too. At present our approach is lopsided.

Tony Little, British headteacher

Little, T (2015) *An Intelligent Person's Guide to Education* (London: Bloomsbury Continuum UK, an imprint of Bloomsbury Publishing Plc.), pp25-26. (See p35 for another quotation from this book). Tony Little was Head Master of Eton (2002-2015) where he himself had been a pupil. (See p67 for another quotation from this book).

~⦿ 35 ⦿~

For many, to be good is to obey parents,
teachers, religious structures, and so on. In fact,
goodness is lived in little ways, loving those
around us daringly and with compassion. To
be good is to be a small wellspring of life.

Jean Vanier (Founder of L'Arche communities)

Vanier, Jean (2016) *Life's Great Questions* (London: SPCK), p49. Jean Vanier has had an extraordinary career which is well worth looking up.

~Q 36 Q~

Childhood is not a race to see how quickly a child can read, write and count. It is a small window of time to learn and develop at the pace that is right for each individual child. Earlier is not better.

Magda Gerber, early childhood educator (d.2007)

Magda Gerber, Hungarian born and French educated, was a US early childhood educator whose approach attracted a large following. Though this quotation is much quoted and printed on colourful posters, I have been unable to find its exact source.

— 37 —

*Children have to be educated, but they have
also to be left to educate themselves.*

Ernest Dimnet (1866-1954)

Ernest Dimnet was a French priest, writer and lecturer whose short book *The Art of Thinking* (first published 1928) had a great impact on many, including John Dewey. http://gutenberg.net.au/ebooks14/1400451h.html, chapter 5 (Accessed 23.12.16).

── 38 ──

*Children aren't colouring books. You don't get
to fill them in with your favourite colours.*

Khaled Hosseini, *The Kite Runner*

Hosseini, K (2004) *The Kite Runner* (London: Bloomsbury Publishing Plc), p19. In a Kabul-based scene early on in the book—and repeated in the film of 2007—these are the words spoken by the family friend, Rahim Khan, to the narrator's father after the latter had been complaining that his young son's character is a disappointment to him. The words were originally passed on to me by a colleague in the NE London School Improvement Service in which we both worked, he having been struck by these words whilst reading the book in a book club to which he belonged.

39

Do all the good you can
By all the means you can.
In all the ways you can.
At all the times you can.
To all the people you can.
As long as ever you can.

Attributed to Charles Wesley (1707-1788)

Though this saying is often attributed to John Wesley—so much so that it is often termed 'John Wesley's "rule of life"'—there is strong evidence to suggest that, though the sentiments might echo much of what he preached, there is no direct use of these precise words in his published works.

40

In compassion and grace, be like the sun
In concealing others' faults, be like the night
In generosity and helping others, be like a river
In anger and fury, be like the dead
In modesty and humility, be like the earth
In tolerance, be like the sea.

Rumi, Persian poet (1207–1273 CE)

Rumi is a poet who appeals to people across many temperamental, cultural and religious divides. This particular text—sometimes curiously called Rumi's 'Seven Advice'—has been reproduced in a wide variety of poster and picture forms (see Google Images).

41

Nobody forgets a good teacher.

Teacher Training Agency slogan, late twentieth century

The 'Teacher Training Agency' was established in September 1994 to be re-launched in September 2005 as the Training and Development Agency for Schools. Later, after having been absorbed into the Department for Education as the Teaching Agency, the latter merged with the National College for School Leadership to become the National College for Teaching and Leadership.

— 42 —

Teaching is a work of heart.

Wall plaque

A little 'twee' perhaps, but I first saw this inscribed saying on the kitchen wall of a friend and colleague of mine who is herself a most gifted (and compassionate) teacher.

~⊘ 43 ⊘~

I touch the future. I teach.

Christa McAuliffe, US Astronaut (1948-1986)

Christa McAuliffe was called 'the first teacher in space' and planned to conduct two lessons from the Challenger space shuttle during its 1986 flight. However, just 73 seconds after lift-off on January 28 1986, the space shuttle exploded and all seven astronauts were killed. A number of US educational facilities, including schools and space centres, have been named in her honour.

44

One could say that without compassion there is no spirituality. One can equally argue, however, that without spirituality compassion would not exist, for compassion forms the bedrock of spiritual practice. Compassion and spirituality are interwoven and integral.

Maurice Irfan Coles, founder of the CoED Foundation

Coles, Maurice I (2015) (ed) *Towards the Compassionate School: From Golden Rule to Golden Thread* (London: Trentham Books), p41.

45

Compassion and love are not mere luxuries. As the source both of inner and external peace, they are fundamental to the continued survival of our species.

The Dalai Lama, Tibetan Buddhist teacher

Since fleeing Tibet in 1959 following the Chinese invasion, the 14th Dalai Lama has become revered by many in the West and elsewhere as a teacher of great perspicacity, compassion and humanity. Dalai Lama (1999), *Ancient Wisdom, Modern World* (London: Little Brown & Co), p139.

Can I see another's woe,
And not be in sorrow too?
Can I see another's grief,
And not seek for kind relief?

From William Blake's poem, 'On Another's Sorrow'

This is the first of nine stanzas of Blake's poem *On Another's Sorrow*. The 'I' of this stanzas is in fact God, the argument that runs through the whole poem being that if people feel sorrow at what they see in the world, how much more does God feel this?

47

So many gods,
So many creeds,
So many paths that wind and wind,
When just the art of being kind
Is all the sad world needs.

Emma Wheeler Wilcox, US poet (1850-1919)

This is the first verse of a three-verse poem entitled 'Voice of the Voiceless'. Emma Wheeler Wilcox was a popular rather than a literary poet. I first heard this verse in January 2017 when a 95 year-old gentleman told me that his mother (born in 1888) was fond of quoting this 'rhyme' to him.

48

Love is something if you give it away,
Give it away, give it away.
Love is something if you give it away,
You end up by having more.

Chorus to Malvina Reynolds' song, Magic Penny

Because of its catchy tune, its ease of learning and its paradoxical love-centred message, the song 'Magic Penny' is a favourite in British primary schools. Malvina Reynolds (1900-1978) was an American song-writer, singer and activist. It is said that she wrote this song in 1949, but not necessarily for children.

49

Academic attainment and exam success can never be more than part of the story of the profound moral responsibility of schools to children, parents, society and the nation ... The work of education, as the linguistic roots suggests, is to 'lead out'. Schools need to lead or draw out of young people all their talents and aptitudes. We cannot and must not define this task purely in terms of academic success.

Anthony Seldon, British educationalist and historian

Seldon, Anthony (2013) *Why the Development of Good Character Matters More Than the Passing of Exams*, the Priestley Lecture (23.1.2013), Jubilee Centre for Character and Virtues, University of Birmingham. http://www.jubileecentre.ac.uk/media/news/article/9/The-Priestley-Lecture-23rd-January-2013 (Accessed 11.2.16).

~~&~~ *50* ~~&~~

We are not engaged, surely, in producing just good performers in the market place or able technocrats. Our task is the training of good human beings, purposeful and wise, themselves with a vision of what it is to be human and the kind of society that makes this possible.

Cardinal Basil Hume (1923-1999)

This passage was cited by the Archbishop of Canterbury, George Carey, at the start of a House of Lords debate on the importance of society's moral and spiritual well-being, particularly the responsibility of schools, on 5 July, 1996. See the text of the Lords Hansard for that date, column 1692. (Accessed 28.2.17)

~~Q 51 Q~~

It is more blessed to give than to receive.

Jesus of Nazareth

These famous words of Jesus cannot be found in any of the Gospel books of the Christian New Testament but were recorded independently by St Luke in his *Acts of the Apostles* (20:35).

~◈ 52 ◈~

*Our happiness is greatest when we contribute
most to the happiness of others.*

Shaker saying

Cited in: Mahoney, K (1993), *Simple Wisdom: Shaker Sayings, Poems and Songs,* (New York, Penguin), p40. An offshoot of the Quakers (Religious Society of Friends), the Shaker movement began when a number of people from Manchester emigrated to the United States in the 18th century. Shaker communities were set up in various parts of the US, though only one very small group exists today. The Shakers stressed the need for simplicity in all that they did whether it was worship, farming or making furniture. (Compare with another Shaker saying, p87).

53

The gift of life is given to us for ourselves and also to bring peace, courage and compassion to others.

John O'Donohue, Irish poet and author (1956-2008)

O'Donohue, John (2000), *Eternal Echoes: Exploring Our Hunger to Belong* (London: Bantam Books), p146.

54

Education is a mirror held against the face of a people. Nations may put on a blustering show of strength to conceal public weakness, erect grand facades to conceal shabby backyards, and profess peace while secretly aiming for conquest, but how they take care of their children tells unerringly who they are.

George Z F Bereday, US educationalist (1920-1983)

Bereday, George Z F (1964) *Comparative Methods in Education* (New York: Holt, Rinehart & Winston), p5.

55

Decisions about what happens in our education systems and schools are inseparable from those about our values, about the kind of society, and world, we want ourselves to be, and about our fundamental ends and purposes as human beings.

Nicholas Tate, British administrator and headteacher

From 'What is education for?', National Education Trust website (www.nationaleducationtrust.net), (accessed October 2006).

56

Seek knowledge and train to be dignified and calm while seeking knowledge, and humble yourselves with those whom you learn from.

Muslim saying

This is sometimes quoted as a saying of the Prophet Muhammad (hadith) but its authenticity is not universally accepted.

— 57 —

Knowledge without wisdom is
like water in the sand.

Sudanese proverb

Posted as 'BBC African proverb of the day' (www.bbc.co.uk/news/world-africa-20884831 (accessed 23.7.16).

~⚬ 58 ⚬~

Buy books and write down knowledge, for
weather is transitory, but knowledge is lasting.

Arab saying

Cited in: Coles, Maurice I (2008) *Every Muslim Child Matters* (Stoke on Trent: Trentham).

59

The unexamined life is not worth living.

Socrates, Greek philosopher (d.399 BCE)

Words, according to Plato, spoken by Socrates at his trial for impiety and corrupting the youth of Athens (see Plato, *Apology,* 38a 5-6).

⟶ 60 ⟵

Until we extend the circle of compassion to all living things, we will not ourselves find peace.

Albert Schweitzer, French-German theologian and doctor
(1875-1965)

From *Kulturphilosopie* (1923), first translated into English as Philosophy of Civilisation in 1949. Albert Schweitzer had a remarkable career as a theologian, musician (his recordings of Bach organ recitals are still obtainable) and, finally, as a medical missionary in Africa.

61

The good life is one inspired by love
and guided by knowledge.

Bertrand Russell, English philosopher (1872-1970)

From *What I Believe* (1925). Bertrand Russell was a prolific writer. For an online collection of over 100 books and articles by Russell, see the Bertrand Russell Society website (http://www.bertrandrussell.org).

— 62 —

The central task of the school must be sensitive, warm, efficient, human, realistic and thorough.

Michael Marland, British educator (1934-2008)

Michael Marland, *Pastoral Care*, 1974; quoted in his Times obituary, 8.7.08.

~Q 63 Q~

Education is the most powerful weapon
we can use to change the world.

Nelson Mandela (1918-2013)

From a speech, 'Lighting your way to a better future', delivered by Nelson Mandela on Wednesday 16 July, 2003, at the University of Witwatersrand Johannesburg, South Africa. http://www.mindset.co.za/ (accessed 4.12.16). This speech was made at the launch of the 'Mindset Network', a not-for-profit organization set up in 2002 to provide educational solutions for formal education and health.

He included this statement in his prepared script but, though he deviated from this script in his actual delivery, he retained these words.

Compassion is a very important aspect of life,
and a fundamental value of human behaviour.

Birmingham school pupil

This statement was one of the outcomes of 'the compassionate comics project' involving 10-11 year-olds which was organized by the CoED Foundation in early 2017. (See p101 for another quotation emanating from this project.)

—⟋ 65 ⟍—

He who by reanimating the old can gain
knowledge of the new is fit to be a teacher.

Confucius, Chinese philosopher and teacher (551-479 BCE)

Analects, 2.11. Cited in Parrinder, G (1990), *Collins Dictionary of Religious and Spiritual Quotations*, (Glasgow: HarperCollins), 62:9.

66

Teachers leave their imprint as much in their attitude to the world as in intellectual approaches.

Michael Gilsenan, US academic

Gilsenan, M (1990), *Recognising Islam,* (New York: I B Tauris), p7.

67

Great teachers use their heads
but teach from the heart.

Tony Little, British headteacher

Little, T (2015) *An Intelligent Person's Guide to Education* (Bloomsbury Continuum UK, an imprint of Bloomsbury Publishing Plc), p48. (See p34 for another quotation from this book.)

— 68 —

One of the most difficult things to give away
is kindness; it usually comes back to you.

Anon

Quoted on the 'Kindness quotes' section of the Random Acts of Kindness Foundation website, www.actsofkindness.org (accessed August 2002).

~~ 69 ~~

I expect to pass through life but once.
If, therefore, there be any kindness I can show,
or any good thing I can do to any fellow being,
let me do it now,
for I shall not pass this way again.

William Penn, British Quaker (1644-1718)

This much-quoted statement was made by one of the early English pioneers who settled in what was later to become the United States of America and after whom the state of Pennsylvania was named.

Wherever there is a human being,
there is an opportunity for kindness.

Seneca, Roman philosopher and dramatist (4BCE-65CE)

The Roman Stoic philosopher, Seneca the Younger, lives on if only through the many vivid and acerbic observations that he made and which are still quoted.

~Q 71 Q~

*What is education? Properly speaking, there
is no such thing as education. Education
is simply the soul of a society as it passes
from one generation to another.*

G K Chesterton, British author (1874-1936)

Observer, 'Sayings of the Week', 6 July 1924.

— 72 —

*One's work may be finished someday
but one's education, never.*

Alexandre Dumas, the Elder (1802-1870)

Cited in Vanzant, I (1993), *Acts of Faith: Daily Meditations for People of Color* (New York: Fireside), March 4.

— 73 —

All of life is education and everybody is a
teacher and everybody is forever a learner.

Abraham Maslow, US psychologist (1908-1970)

Maslow, Abraham (1954) *Motivation and Personality* (Harper & Row). I first saw this quotation – in a shortened form, 'All of life is education ... everybody is forever a learner' – on a poster at the University of Warwick Institute of Education in May 2007.

~~&~~ 74 ~~&~~

*I have never been able to let the phrase 'deliver
the curriculum' cross my lips. I will teach it,
I might even "instruct" children, but delivery
is strictly for Postman Pat. Yet some people
absorb fresh terms like a sponge, partly because
it is thought to sound smart and up-to-date,
and partly from willingness to conform.*

Ted Wragg, British educationalist and academic (1938-2005)

From 'The Last Word' in The Times Educational Supplement, 28 February, 2002. Ted Wragg was a towering presence in British education, his weekly column 'The Last Word' seeking to challenge much of what was being said in the educational field, until his untimely death in 2005.

75

That which discloses to the wise and disguises from the foolish their lack of understanding.

❦

Definition of 'Education' in the Devil's Dictionary

Bierce, Ambrose (2001) *The Enlarged Devil's Dictionary* (London: Penguin), p105. Ambrose Bierce (1842-c.1914?) was a US journalist and newspaper editor who delighted in penning sardonic and witty 'definitions' of well-known words. For a modern take on this approach, see p82.

~ 76 ~

It is in the shelter of each other that the people live.

Traditional Irish saying

Some people are so attached to particular sayings that they even place them at the bottoms of letters or emails. This one was seen at the bottom of an email from an academic at Stranmillis University College, Belfast (July 2014). It greatly echoes the African concept of Ubuntu (see notes on p11 & p77).

77

*It's through someone
that someone becomes somebody.*

African saying

The idea behind this saying is sometimes referred to as the African concept of Ubuntu. This version was given to me by a Ghanaian. The concept of Ubuntu, with or without direct reference to the term Ubuntu, is often referred to by Desmond Tutu: see his statement p11.

— 78 —

You never really understand a person until you consider things from his point of view—until you climb into his skin and walk around in it.

Harper Lee, US author

Lee, H, *To Kill a Mockingbird,* published by William Heinemann, reprinted by permission of The Random House Group Limited. Interestingly, the supposition that we can actually 'stand in the shoes' of other people and so understand their worlds is much contended within social scientific circles.

~⟨ 79 ⟩~

For many pupils establishing relationships of respect and care is a necessary foundation for intellectual as well as social development.

Hargreaves and Fullan (1998)

Hargreaves, A & Fullan, M (1998) *What's Worth Fighting For in Education?* (Buckingham: Open University Press), p32.

── 80 ──

I always knew that deep down in every human heart, there was mercy and generosity. No one is born hating another person because of the colour of his skin, or his background, or his religion. People must learn to hate, and if they can learn to hate, then they can be taught to love. For love comes more naturally to the human heart than its opposite.

Nelson Mandela, former President of South Africa
(1918-2013)

A comb through the many Internet quotation collections shows that this statement from the very end of Nelson Mandela's autobiography usually omits the first sentence given here ('I always knew... mercy and generosity'). Given the nature of this book, however, it was felt important to include it. Mandela, Nelson (1994) *Long Walk to Freedom* (London: Little, Brown and Company), p615.

81

Leadership is always important. At great social turning points it is more important than ever. At times like these, the leadership we need is not leadership that turns us against others or holds us back in awe. It is leadership that lifts us up and turns us around together in pursuit of a common cause that expresses and advances our humanity.

Andy Hargreaves and Dennis Shirley, *The Fourth Way*

Hargreaves, A and Shirley, D (2009), *The Fourth Way: The Inspiring Future for Educational Change* (Thousand Oaks, CA: Corwin).

82

One who colludes in a nation's arrangements
for the stultification of its children.

⚜

Definition of 'educator' in *The Devil's Dictionary of Education.*

Burgess, Tyrrell (2002) *The Devil's Dictionary of Education* (Bloomsbury Continuum, an imprint of Bloomsbury Publishing Plc), p49. The antecedent to statements of this mordant style was, of course, Ambrose Bierce's famous *Devil's Dictionary* published in the US towards the end of the nineteenth century (see p75). Burgess dedicates his own collection to 'the victims of education everywhere'.

~ 83 ~

Schools are not about enabling children to have a
living but about children being able to have a life.

Elliot Eisner, US educationalist (1933-2014)

This quotation was excitedly passed on to me in 1998 by a colleague who had just been to a London lecture by Elliot Eisner who was Professor of Art and Education at the Stanford Graduate School of Education.

84

It appears increasingly challenging for schools to think about anything other than short-term gains to short-term outcomes. The deeper thinking about the purpose and the development of those values and skills that are at the heart of SMSC*, and that are anything but soft, has been rendered far more difficult by the constantly changing terrain of policy initiatives and the attendant focus on narrow priorities.

Schools with Soul (2014)
[*spiritual, moral, social and cultural education]

Peterson, A, Lexmond, J, Hallgarten, J, Kerr, D *Schools with Soul: A new approach to Spiritual, Moral, Social and Cultural Education –* Executive Summary (London: RSA: 2014), p1.

_~& 85 &~_

Students learn through the eyes of a smiling teacher.

Anon

Quoted by a contributor during a conference focusing on Emotionally Literate Schools, organised by Antidote (Campaign for Emotional Literacy), Church House, Westminster, May 2002.

86

I have learned much from my teachers,
even more from my colleagues, but I have
learned the most from my students.

Jewish Talmud, Ta'anit 7a

Cited in: Mahoney, K (1993), *Simple Wisdom: Shaker Sayings, Poems and Songs* (New York: Penguin), p48.

87

Begin today! No matter how feeble the light,
let it shine as best it may. The world may need
just that quality of light which you have.

Shaker saying

Cited in: Mahoney, K (1993), *Simple Wisdom: Shaker Sayings, Poems and Songs* (New York: Penguin), p48. (Compare with another Shaker saying, p52)

~❧ 88 ❧~

*More than anything else, more than expectations,
passionate engagement or standards, teaching
is about hope. Every child is one teacher's hope
for the future ... Hope should never disappear
... Hope is the ultimate virtue on which a
decent and successful school system depends.*

Hargreaves and Fullan (1998)

Hargreaves, A and Fullan, M (1998) *What's Worth Fighting for in Education* (Buckingham: Open University Press), p61.

89

Simplicity, patience, compassion.
These three things are your greatest treasures.

Simple in actions and thoughts,
you return to the source of being.

Patient with both friends and enemies,
you accord with the way things are.

Compassion toward yourself,
you reconcile all beings in the world.

Lao Tzu, *Tao Te Ching*

This much-quoted text is the 4th verse of the classic Chinese Taoist (pronounced Dow-ist) text, the *Tao Te Ching*, parts of which probably date back to the 4th century BCE.

90

Respect the dignity and inherent worth of all human beings, regardless of their station in life or outer accomplishments, and you will respect yourself.

Laurence Boldt, US self-help author

Boldt, L G (1997), *Zen Soup*, (New York: Penguin), p86.

We are far more united and have far more in common with each other than things that divide us.

Jo Cox, Labour MP (2015)

Jo Cox, the member of parliament for Batley and Spen, rose to international fame when she was murdered whilst carrying out constituency business in June 2016. This quotation is taken from her maiden speech delivered in the House of Commons in June 2015.

~ 92 ~

Life is best when you build bridges between people,
not walls.

Billy Crystal at Muhammad Ali's funeral, June 2016

From Billy Crystal's eulogy to Muhammad Ali, June 2016.
Quoted in the Guardian, 13.6.16, p25.

93

Education in common human weakness and vulnerability should be a very profound part of the education of all children. Children should learn to be tragic spectators and to understand with subtlety and responsiveness the predicaments to which human life is prone.

M C Nussbaum (2014)

Nussbaum, M C (2014) 'Compassion and terror' in M Ure and M Frost (eds) *The Politics of Compassion* (London: Routledge), p204.

94

Hard times make you bitter or make you more compassionate. Choosing love at each crossroads helps you come out the other side, not as a damaged person, but as an exceptional one.

Jewel Kilcher, US singer, actress and author

This quotation was displayed on the US website of Wisdom 2.0, an organisation that describes itself as 'the premier gathering exploring living mindfully in the digital age'. (www.wisdom2summit. com: accessed 2.1.17)

95

To experience is to learn.

Aeschylus, *Agamemnon*

The classical scholar who passed on this statement from Aeschylus, the ancient Greek tragedian (525-456 BCE), added the following note: another translation could be 'Wisdom comes through suffering'. The Greek word pathein, to suffer, to experience, is the one from which we get 'passion', in every sense, including the religious.

~⚬ 96 ⚬~

Learning is a bitter root, but it bears sweet fruit.

Czech proverb

Cited in: Mieder, Wolfgang (1998) *Illuminating Wit, Inspiring Wisdom: Proverbs From Around the World* (Paramus, NJ: Prentice Hall Press), p131. Mieder (born 1944)—professor of German and folklore at the University of Vermont, USA—is widely considered to be the world's greatest living proverb scholar.

Your worst enemy is your best teacher.

The Buddha

This is a much-quoted Buddhist teaching which is typically Buddhist in that it invites us to look through commonly accepted ideas and 'truths'. The Dalai Lama uses this teaching when he says, for example, 'We can even come to appreciate that those who cause us difficulty are providing us with the opportunity to develop tolerance' (*An Open Heart: Practising Compassion in Everyday Life* [London: Hodder & Stoughton, 2001], p123).

98

Teach your children how to forgive;
make your homes places of love and forgiveness;
make your streets and neighbourhoods
centres of peace and reconciliation.

Pope John Paul II following an attempt on his life (1981)

Cited in: Panati, C (1999), *Words to Live By*, (New York: Penguin), p289.

— 99 —

Instruction in youth is like engraving in stones.

Moroccan proverb

Westermarck, Edward (1931) *Wit and Wisdom in Morocco* (New York: Horace Liveright), p290. The author—a Finnish sociologist, philosopher and anthropologist (1862-1939)—describes this particular proverb as being 'widespread'.

100

Teaching kids to count is fine,
but teaching them what counts is best.

Bob Talbert, US columnist (1936-1999)

This statement by Bob Talbert, a Chicago-based columnist, is much repeated in Internet quotation websites (though, curiously, his surname is sometimes given as 'Tarber'). I have been unable to trace the exact source, however.

If we didn't have compassion,
what would life be like?

Birmingham school pupil

This statement was one of the outcomes of 'the compassionate comics project' involving 10–11 year-olds which was organized by the CoED Foundation in early 2017. (See p64 for another quotation emanating from this project.)

Afterword

Compassion has gone viral in the 21st century! In no small part this is due to advances in the science and neuroscience of compassion that empirically validate ancient contemplative and spiritual wisdom that maintained (to use modern jargon) that we are all wired for compassion. The problem is that we are not hard-wired because our brains respond to both positive and negative stimuli and build neural pathways based upon these experiences. In short, the more compassionate you are, the more compassionate you become. The obverse is equally true!

The CoED Foundation, an English charity (what in the USA is called a 501(c) 3) was founded in 2012 to help schools and other institutions build compassionate cultures which promote the hard-wiring of these drives. In its relatively short life, it has produced a range of materials, supporting articles, projects, the first in a series of comics, and a seminal book, *Towards the Compassionate School: From Golden Rule to Golden Thread*.

We are delighted and so grateful that Dr Bill Gent, one of our trustees, has taken the time and trouble to produce this, our second book. His selection captures the very essence of compassionate education in a manner which resonates with everyone, not just professional educators. The Foundation hopes you find it a useful addition to the growing body of material dedicated to creating a secure, caring and happy future for young people everywhere.

For further information, please visit our website: www.coedfoundation.org.uk.

Maurice Irfan Coles
CEO, the CoED Foundation

Index of names of people to whom sayings and quotations have been attributed

www.ingramcontent.com/pod-product-compliance
Lightning Source LLC
Chambersburg PA
CBHW051812040426
42446CB00007B/640